POEMS FOR THE HEART AND THE SUN

POEMS
FOR
THE HEART
AND THE SUN

BY

ANTHONY PANZARDI

LEGAS

Edited by J.A. Tully

Poems for the Heart and the Sun, by Anthony Panzardi
ISBN 978-1-939693-33-4

Library of Congress Control Number: 2018960667

The author has also published six other books of poetry with Legas:

Auriga, Between Yellow Night and Refractive Sea, 1999;
Horologium, Beyond Tangible Dreams and Unconscious Walls, 2005;
Poems of Themes and Unity, 2010;
Poems for the Twenty-First Century, 2013;
Poems for the Lost Millennium, 2015;
Selected Poems of Anthony Panzardi, 2016.

For information and for orders, write to:

Legas

P.O. Box 149
Mineola, New York
11501, USA

3 Wood Aster Bay
Ottawa, Ontario
Canada K2R1D3

Legaspublishing.com

Table of Contents

JUST A STONE AND NOTHING MORE

Compassion or the solitary tree,
A short declivity,
And a long winding road barely touching the human skin,
Barely touching the jackal's den,
And the moths in daylight dripping with wing and decay,
Dripping along the out-stretched eye,
Visiting the lamp or the bluff,
A strand covered in scarlet sea,
Liquid sand gurgling like foam,
An opening for the human mind,
A warning for the jackal's home,
And the philosophy sign embedded before the black sand.
But I felt the jackal's breath on my jaw,
A flowery heat,
Rancid,cold like the human skin,
Flat like the distant plains,
Leveled like the cities of land,
And the measuring guide, without pages or plans,
Without a limit or an edge,
And the small brown shapes in flight,
Avoiding the subhuman hands,
Visiting the open flame.
But I sensed the dog's whimper at my door,
A hollow pitch, morbid, still like the solitary tree,
Vertical like the sudden leaf,
Brief like the breath of existence,
And the cruel peak's curl,
Imitating the cold pup's blanket,
Imitating a blanket of darkness,
And the only stone floats upon the bright sea,
A gradual separation or permanent like the far ends of night,
And the only brightness fades from the distant stars,
A separation without color or dimension,
A white dog under the geometrical tree,
More whimpering in the corners of the light.
But I realized the outside elements, a gradual separation,
Subtle and permanent to the individual mind,
Horizontal like the sudden Earth,

Brief like the breath of existence,
A whole new logic of separation with thought and stone,
Like a human thought hidden behind the tree,
Or Earth's air hidden behind the stone,
And the days that we live are like a piece and a puzzle,
Visiting our thoughts and the air,
Waiting among what is probable or not,
Imitating the elements for the survival sign,
Or slowly moving the lamp along the out-stretched eye,
A warning for the countless stones.

AND THE SKY SEEMED LIKE A CHILD

And the rain became the tears
As the clouds swell into the gray sky,
And the albatross, white between plumage and air,
Circles the salty rain,
Absorbed into the gray and the glare,
Soaring behind the empty heights,
Or the beauty behind the hollow face
As the clear blue petals fall like the salty rain,
And the innocence of the sky lost between the clouds and the gray,
Lost between the tears and the rain,
And when the laughter stopped among the stratosphere,
The small azure spread across cradle and exosphere,
A vast aperture, barely enough for pupil and tear,
And the soft blue hue spread across like a shadow over the hollow face,
Or the beauty fell behind the rugged hue,
An innocent blue changing between day and night,
A blackness between child and sky,
A departure between troposphere and exosphere,
A vast beginning, barely enough to compensate for the small azure,
And the tender minds susceptible to a vast conclusion.

CHESS AT DAWN AND SOLITAIRE AT DUSK

The voice below a strategic range felt thin and dry
As a red panda moves clockwise around the dry white fog,
The thin Earth, flat, or round between mind or sphere,
The crepuscular wake heard between a thin dry voice,
But when the night faded with time
And the sole survivor stood between the two stars,
A small somber hand reached for the only light,
A single star in the western hemisphere,
Without a center or a rim,
Without structure or purpose,
With rising and setting as a misconception,
A tragic shape between east and west,
A blue shadow playing the game with pawn and card,
An empty space between the crepuscular light,
And the sole survivor weeped or wept between the two stars,
Or they wept below the voice
As a black lion moved counterclockwise around the red morning dusk.

BALLAD OF THE HUMAN BEING

I

When the dust took the shape of life,
And the breath shaped the posthumous song,
An infinite cry began before dawn and death,
Before the cognitive mind,
Before the fire imbued the awe in man,
A primitive cry under winter's leaves,
Or white buds under frozen boughs,
And Earth shed its heart,
A nakedness of soil,
A transparentness of sea,
A blinding night guided by life and fear,
Or unknown trees under the western sky,
But the purpose became lost, again, among specks and brains,
And the whole reason became a primitive song,
An infinite cry among the scent of skin and snakes,
Among the billions of solitary tracks,
Or the naked shape, transparent behind white buds and unknown trees,
Running against the shadows of stars,
Running with the speck of glare,
Running away from the reason and the song,
Or the shape became the flesh and the nakedness became the serpent.

II

When the sky took the shape of night,
And the eye shaped the predawn fear,
A strange sound began behind the dwindling flame,
And the mind began to think of dust and void,
Or the old man regressed into the womb,
A pre-birth under the trauma of night,
And Earth shed its heart,
And the dust shed its hue,
Or the wind mixed time and space,
An inaudible cry began beyond the human mind,
Beyond the empty sky,
Before the birth of man,

11

Before the lights of night,
Or the first star took the shape of light,
And the old man compared heart and night,
An Earth-ridden life crippled by the cognitive mind,
A desperate attempt for breath and birth,
A life span measured with the manmade watch,
Measured between day and night,
Measured without the knowledge of void,
And the human began to think about the dust,
Or the posthumous cry sounded like the last shade of dust and light.

III

When the flesh took the shape of death,
And the heart shaped the post-war dust,
A silent rain began between Earth and man,
And a voiceless journey began in the lightless womb,
Or a microscopic extinction of thoughts and perpetual time,
And when the fall shaped the setting sun,
Man crawled on belly and tongue,
Seeking the sound of the rising sun,
Striving for the peaks and the plots,
Praying without hands to the thunder and the light,
Weeping without eyes below the horizontal moon,
And the old human crawled like man on belly and tongue,
Waiting for the ultimate force to make a subtle change in light or thoughts,
Waiting for the inevitable sign among beauty and horror,
Or the garden blocked by the serpent's hand,
Impenetrable by brain and tail,
A nakedness of skin and stars,
An ultimate fear of change and light,
Or an ultimate fear of finite thoughts buried among the finite soil.
The cognitive mind at dawn took the shape of a human being
Or took the shape of life and dust.

THE LAST FEAST BEFORE THE FINAL SETTING

A celebration took place
Before the zephyr became a gentle breeze,
And before the tree became a permanent sound,
And before the hungry leopard perched upon the lion's bones,
But on the hill's impregnable shade,
A social cry beckoned from the comfort zone,
A tranquil sleep echoed from the busy street,
But among all the pyres and plates,
The first clouds rise or the warning signs fall,
Like a dark fog rolling over bright days,
A premature celebration between humans and Earth,
Or food and wine served too late between the hour and the birth,
Served on dirt while the moths fly like vast yellow birds,
Intercepting a primeval thought,
Blocking a vast image of an omnipotent breeze,
Or a future celebration took place after life vanished from the sea
And after the wolf perched upon the fox's bones,
But they ate and drank and toasted with a speech for mankind,
Torn between the tears and the laughter.

IT IS JUST LIKE FALLING BENEATH THE RIM OF PARADISE

The invisible wall shaped the timeless edge,
And the children sat at the edge of the cliff,
Or I saw the brontosaurus and they saw the apatosaurus,
And the valley became a vertical path,
A vision trapped between the mind and the eyes,
A thought trapped between the heavens and Earth,
Or I saw the indefinite circle,
A dead end falling below the rimless curve,
And they walk peacefully between the trees and the stones,
Collecting the seeds and the sand,
Hearing the perfect circle of the stars altering their natural course,
But I understood the brevity of life,
The clarity of death,
The grayness of breath,
The uncertainty of a beating heart,
And the omnipresence of space and inevitability,
Or an endless view, horizontal from sun to shore,
But they stood beyond the invisible wall,
Looking for the missing clues,
Looking for the air between sun and shore,
And I felt the closeness of the void,
Or a beautiful particle of sand and brine,
A massive glow from the rimless edge,
A timeless edge visible in the past tense,
And I moved cautiously between twigs and pebbles,
Analyzing the past and the future,
Watching the planet rise below the air-shaped surface,
Hearing the five senses grow silent behind the empty light,
But the wall shaped the circular edge,
A time line for the weeping sky,
A clear rain behind the gray sun,
Or a great fall in a troubled stream.

THREE WHITE BIRDS ON FOUR BLACK BRANCHES

With the extinction of feathers and leaves,
I hibernate in the open space,
Coiled around the shrouded air,
Standing face up against the grizzled stump,
Protruding under the sun like an egg or a bud,
And with the exception of wings and roots,
The crowd disappears in the open space,
Extruding among the entire Earth,
Showing the entire space of limbs and beaks,
And with the vast distance of night,
I walked alone in the light,
Keeping an uneven pace with life,
Trying to catch a glimpse at the hidden sky,
And I remembered the mathematical flaw or the grayness of setting,
A fragment on the open road,
And I remembered the feathers and the leaves,
Or a lonely walk in the light,
Keeping an uneven pace with the warmth and the cold,
Trying desperately to avoid the hollowed ground,
Or trying hopelessly to face the daytime moon,
And worried about the math and the color.

IN THE DIMENSION OF A CONTINUITY OF THOUGHTS

In the darkness of the unconscious,
The ape introduces himself as man
And chatters uncontrollably under the solar eclipse,
But I rationalized my existence when the phenomenon was over,
Or when the correlation ceased between the two,
And the transition seemed to linger for the ultimate amount,
An unmeasurable phase destined for inevitability,
But I rationalized my being as the conciseness of that existence,
Or when the white rose becomes dust
And my words suffer the ultimate neglect,
I will lie on the thorn and the earth,
Or I will introduce myself as man
And think analytically under the chronological bridge,
But the water did not seek its level,
Flowing in a state of matter,
Flowing in a state of mind,
And I visited the only place in the world,
Every aspect of thought,
Every atom of mankind,
The only place between the two,
A few steps between the next spot,
And my decision was vast when the uncertainty was over.

THE UNAVOIDABLE DEATH AND THE DESTINY OF LIFE

Out near the mirror's light
A daylight shade covers the unborn earth,
A soil so deep that we walk toward the green and white hills,
Crawling toward the white wall,
Raising human-like arms between the breath-like air,
Touching anything tangible before the final breath,
And they witnessed the trauma of birth,
The crucifixion of seeds
And the resurrection of earth,
Or covered in the daylight shade,
The hyenas walk toward the white hill,
Breathing heavily on the invisible peak,
And I signaled the unborn tree
That it might grow beneath the solitary cloud,
Waiting for rain beneath the limb and the shade,
Or I longed for the green and white hills,
Sitting motionless on the invisible peak,
Thinking about the life span of seeds and Earth,
Reflecting on the mirror and the light,
Judging the similarities in humanity,
Or the difference in time.

WHILE TRAVELING ALONE THROUGH SPACE AND TIME

They picked the flowers, bright and blue,
Firmly rooted in sand,
Vast like the dying star or moist like the weeping eye,
Inspecting the view of reality, the void, and themselves,
Or they picked the earth, thick and brown,
Shoveling out the weeds under the bright blue star,
Or the wild dogs crying under profundity and collar,
But I saw them recede past nose and tail,
Mimicking the flood and the mist,
Or they waited for the sign,
Overwhelmed by silence,
Struggling to count the words,
Misunderstood by phases of the moon,
But I saw them recently flying the heavy kite,
Predicting the outcome of gravity and man,
Or they waited under the awning,
Overwhelmed by the flowers,
But the image seemed fictitious,
Like a storybook for tots or tyrants,
It seemed predictable and real,
An empty likeness of oneself,
A countless vision of strange faces staring inanely at flowers and stars,
But I see the pointless shapes behind the painted rocks,
Reupholstering the couch and re-editing psychoanalysis,
Or they fell prematurely into the twinkling petals,
Far removed from history and galaxy,
A short distance from the probability or the unconscious,
And I know the equation is a fragment,
Moving from here to there,
Comparing the flat side of Earth,
Identifying them from reality,
Living in the corner with infinite room.

THE PHILOSOPHERS RECLINE BENEATH THE HAMMOCK AND THE BLACK HOLE

Where the tiglons graze thin under the spreading guise,
The citizens, from tree and shore,
Gather their life up piecemeal
Before the reign of light closes its manmade core.
And I stood alone between dust and door.
And the citizens stood together among center and yawn,
But the tracks were not human or made at the side of the wall,
A recent blemish made under hair a time ago,
A multitude of skin and ideas far-reaching a subconscious plan,
But the huge heavy cats were seen hiding behind bedding and blackness,
And I spoke, from tree and shore,
Where my voice could not be heard,
Making my presence known in geometrical form,
Searching for the tracks now buried under the wall,
Trying to reason with the unkempt minds,
Collecting the unsymmetrical spaces at the side of the wall,
But the right angle was covered with grass,
Each blade slain by the sharp wind,
Each wind counted by civilization,
Or a logical form buried behind the manmade door.
And I listened to the prone position,
Or the empirical form buried between the tracks and the wall,
Not thinking below the reign of light,
But the old feline rejects losing its stripes or mane.

ISOLATION WITH THE SAME SHAPE AS IO

Invisible, impenetrable sight,
Magnificent along the eastern sky,
Alone at the foothill,
The oreodont vocalized silently at the oval shale,
And I read about it next to the book or the drought,
An abundance of water and clarity,
And I floated on the sandstone,
Elliptical next to the dryness,
Uncomfortable in the surroundings,
Underestimated below the bright slope,
But the dead were not in plain view,
They were next to the tiny foothill,
Apart from the segregation and orientation,
In the vicinity of the cold orbit,
But I imitated the inertia with respect for the dead,
Or I blinked next to the book and the drought,
Infinitely still in the human spectrum,
The whole nonexistence of form was blown away by the impenetrable day,
And the sphere-like day suddenly became the unconscious form,
An army of ghosts after a long sleep,
A ghost-like form that existed upon the wakeful hour,
A mindful day of questions and forms,
And I asked about the day and the hour,
Or the whole part was answered in the dark by the index and the trained
oreodont.

THE BIRDS AND THE BATS

Light...
Over Earth and wings
Moved slowly under bosom and pate,
Or I moved the roost the best I could,
Leaving it partially in the solar phase,
Near a gentle tree split by sheath and shell,
But the climate maintained its quadruple tone,
Altered by the night and the glare,
Or I began to remember the whole process of life within the measured
                              plan,
Like a submerged dream sleeping in the open air,
The psychological convergence of a twilight span,
And the bright cave attached to the blackness,
A deep unconscious sight of the two that combined,
Or they moved visibly uncertain about the obvious transition,
Speaking to the same metamorphosis just before sunrise.
And they sang noticeably toward the subtle change,
Speaking indirectly to me about the universe and the four wings,
Singing to the same flight just before sundown,
Or I moved along the convergence of life,
A deep unconscious sight of the light over Earth and wings
                              ...Darkness.

THE PENSIVE MOOD OF THE STARS AND THE DAYTIME MOON

I wore the remnants of civilization
Close to my heart,
A vest of soil and stem,
An atmospheric bond caked with Earth,
A stone-scented coat opened for the light,
And I wore the colors of Earth like the garments of man,
Alone and afraid like a primitive ape contemplating death.
But I saw the beauty of life in the light of the stars,
Or in the reflection of the yellow moon,
And I became a piece of the mood,
A fragment of the whole being,
A piece of Earth, a living being,
Alone and afraid below the beautiful sun,
Or the chamois settling parallel to the only side of the fence and the rain,
Exclaiming to a vein-scented beast by settling near flood and space.
But I studied the tablets in vain,
Turning it like a petrified book,
Trying to bend the pages of knowledge,
Trying to read the words under the night sky,
Or the Zanzibar leopard running parallel to the only radiant spot in
                                                  existence,
Running parallel to the flood and the rain.
But I remembered the definition of a philosophical word,
A translation from parchment to stone,
A philosophical plea directed above,
A language destined to fall.

NOTHINGNESS TURNED A SLENDER STEM INTO A GREAT BOUGH

In a fading forest like the gray city,
A blurry face, void of recognition,
Lowers its eyes upon the white sea,
And the towering land reflects its ripples,
But the stage is set on a vanishing hill,
A close encounter like the black setting.
And I turned toward the ground,
Realizing its significance,
Trying to penetrate the sky,
Trying to penetrate humanity,
Trying to understand the dead.
And the stage was leveled according to the time,
A brief encounter like the purple dawn.
But I concentrated on the earth,
Observing its layers under the sky,
Peeling the beautiful blue within my mind,
Trying to warn another human being of its significance,
Or the late flowers lying on the fetal side,
Covered in early snow,
Or I played a mind game with nature and the dead,
But we were caught in the midst of life,
Struggling to reach that slender bough,
A hairline crack under the great mind,
And so the ground turned over,
Disturbed by the ripples of Earth,
Or the great hail of void.
But I concentrated on the mist,
Observing its layers under the sky,
Peeling the lost time within my mind,
Trying to warn the stone of its significance,
Or the cold fruit hanging on the darker side,
Covered in human saliva,
Or the blurry life I once knew.

BEYOND THE LIGHT OF DANTE'S COMEDY

I

Suffering as a solid on the symmetrical orb,
Or they pulled the heavy load ahead of the blaze and the circular turn,
A difficult choice made in haste,
Surrounded by the rim of the flame,
Waiting for two oceans or the incomplete cloud,
Synchronizing as they pulled the heavy strings with burning hands,
An indefinite sign among the lowest ground,
Searching blindly for the symmetrical treetop or the spherical azure.

II

Indifference as a liquid on the saturated plain,
Or they pushed the long burden behind the snowbank and the circular line,
A hasty choice made between the rock or the stone,
Surrounded by the depth of the frost,
Waiting for the two clouds or the complete horizon,
Reconstructing the middle of an old tree with frozen hands,
A probable sign near the gray mound,
Speaking before dusk at the saturated hole or the towering soil.

III

The dead as a gas lying in the supine position below the unconquered star,
Or they lived on the face of Earth,
An inevitable choice made by an unknown force,
Surrounded by the burst of air,
Waiting for the birth of an atom or a thought,
Predicting the future of matter with invisible hands,
An inanimate sign behind the remote parturition,
Standing brain deep in the animate haze or the recurrent scene.

IV

The resurrection as plasma on the unconscious world,
Or they slept among the luster and laughter.

COGITO ERGO SUM?

I thought it will be the past
When the white crow lands and divides upon the empty skulls,
And I thought the cerebral music sounded like the existence on Earth,
Or to populate the moon with philosophers and guests,
But I thought I was right near the dirt and the stars,
Near the dregs and the sun,
But I thought I was right from the white horizon to the ashen bud,
Or I waited impatiently for the pause,
Where my thoughts were for the future,
A reflection of my estimation,
A predictable error in my judgment,
Off from the pause and the start,
Standing at the finish line below the nestling and the skyline,
Standing naked or incognito,
Thinking about my mind and thoughts,
Admitting to Earth about the pause and death,
Deciding whether to talk or turn at the start,
Unable to reach a conclusion between thinking and tangibility,
But I stopped guessing about the past,
Or I waited patiently for the birth,
Where my thoughts did not exist,
A subjective guess at my estimation,
A predictable error in our judgment,
Off like a bulb or a star,
No beginning or end?
And the pause had nothing to do with my thoughts,
Or it will be the future when death becomes inevitable.

A FINE LINE BETWEEN DENEB AND DUST?

I followed the dim light between light and twilight,
And I followed the sound between the northern spot and the trampled
mud,
Or the earth was planted instead of seeds behind a horizontal tree,
But I followed an imaginary line,
A visible pattern toward an empty hole,
A visible line between the past and the light,
But I followed the empty light toward an underground gleam,
Or I stood involuntarily under the night and the nebula,
Where my motions were for the future,
A reflection of my probability,
An unpredictable length in my life span,
Off from the mountain and the grave,
Standing in the past below the foot and the edge,
Standing petrified or invisible,
Thinking about reality and fantasy,
Admitting to myself about the past and the future,
Deciding whether to observe or touch the ground,
Unable to reach a conclusion between sound and trees,
But I continued guessing about the day,
Or I sat voluntarily under the oak,
Where my perception became acute,
A predictable outcome in our judgment,
Off like insanity or rationality,
No belief or truth.
And the night had nothing to do with the nebula,
Or it will be the perception of time when reality becomes inevitable.

TILL DEATH DO US PART?

The obsequies of the cumulus clouds
Descending behind a movable stone,
Or the interment of the shoreline declining
Before a lamented rose,
But I positioned myself between the bud and the boulder,
Frightened between the departure of rain and sand,
Remaining still in the foreground near the peach trees,
Or my palms felt like blossoms and bark,
A thumb and wrist strange in the background near the buried pit,
But I positioned the soil far from the clouds or the beach,
Their beauty in full view before the entry of man,
Before the interim of life and death,
But I organized the soil above the beach and beside the clouds,
Watching Uranus go through the lens of the eye,
Or watching the ape and the fish stop on the calm of the storm,
As an illogical configuration forms behind the impenetrable order,
So when the transformation became a reality,
I noticed a subtle change in the position and organization,
Or a profound study of the unknown toward an obvious transition.

BLESSED ARE THE MEEK:
FOR THEY SHALL INHERIT THE EARTH?

The bright-skinned light of the bulging sun
Beats down upon the dark terrain,
And the dun and tawny peaks
Wilt in the tender eyes,
Or the rotation missed its turn around the pallid star,
And the army of haze showed its husk and shell,
Showing the eyes and the terrain,
Sculpting itself around the inherent mind,
But I weighed the tough and tender land,
Unbalanced by scales and scars,
Unbalanced by the measurement of time,
A process of elimination from below and base,
A fragment of the feeble mind,
Turning itself around the modern land,
But I balanced the scales and scars,
Weighed by the elimination of time,
Or the mighty scab placed on husk and shell,
A thick crust on the planet's thin skin,
A dead vegetation watered down by tearful eyes,
A blind geneticist tending the garden under the pallid sun,
But I appraised the significance of Earth or the deep geological faults,
Leaning on the proportion of life,
Comparing the husk and the seed,
Comparing the turtle and the egg.

WHAT THE LEAVES SAID
A POEM IN ONE ACT

GOD: Wouldst thou grow between the beginning and dawn, and stand with life toward the heavens, extending thy boughs of edible birth or flourish Earth with exquisite hue created in the time before man and beast, taking in their lungs and skin, sharing this land, existing on this Earth in peace and plentitude with thyself and thy kind. But throughout the time thine use is for birth and repose by beast and crucifixion and profit by man, but thou art here in this place without reproach or sin.

TREE: Thy name I know, a supreme force of cognition and all that exists, the ultimate sign of rain and light, an existence immeasurable from the first seed of life or the pit from the beginning of the void, thy name be above all that ever lived, a name called by the celestial thunder, even the mighty wind shivers from thy omnipotence. But I ask thee, then and now, among the mist of the garden and the modern city, is it the sin of man or beast?

GOD: Yea, 'tis the sin of man unto Earth and unto himself. I hath given him dominion over all on Earth, a role that time hath proven a false god, from all the days of fig leaves to fire or flood. What lesson will learn this cognitive mind? A lesson to forsake all his dominion, an Earth of land and sea, an Earth of flora and fauna.

TREE: But was I the source of sin, the origin of this foul deed, a shelter for this verbal act? I grew in the midst of man and beast, from seed to sky, under white moon and yellow sun, above the earth and the dead, a provider of fruit for all to share with beast and man. But I long sensed the wicked climate, a constant stir from crown to roots, not the kind from snow or drought, but from a vigilance of man's strides.

GOD: Thou art not of shame, 'tis of the field and the earth in which man walks and begets that the seed burst forth, a stain upon the clouds and the stars.

TREE: I feel all the flora as my kind. I feel us all as one as the yellow sun my strength and the white moon my rest, and I feel the beast

29

in my proximity, but man I fear even beyond the light-year.

GOD: Here is thy place on Earth with thy kind and all that exists under the heavens, grow tall and multiply, let thy limbs hang heavy, and let the waters nourish thy roots.

TREE: Days were good in the beginning with the birth of light, and the darkness filled with the birth of stars, and the petals covered the vast land, shedding the seasons in countless forms. But then came a change in time with dust and breath, an image of flesh and bone, a tiller of day and night.

GOD: Thou question my design of dust, my breath for the living soul?

TREE: Nay, I fear for all the beasts and all my kind. We use the form of Earth to survive and multiply. But man hath altered that form, shaping Earth unto his own kind.

GOD: 'Tis true, by the two great lights and its division of day and night, and by all the firmament from void unto creation.

TREE: 'Tis my existence, under the pale yellow light and the vast new moon, and by all the firmament from void unto man. 'Tis my fate.

A QUADRILLION IN THE AMOUNT
OF AN ABSENT HUE

Far from the human eye,
A transparent shade settled upon the human mind,
And the gray bird settled upon the broken rock,
And the megatherium was in the shape of its first habitat,
A modification of a number pattern,
An addition of everything perceived on a non-human level,
Or the citizens could sit waiting for the change in shape,
A modification of a gray rock,
Or the citizens could sit upon the transparent shade,
Waiting for the change to take place,
Waiting for the amount to make sense,
Collecting the sequence of thoughts from the beginning to the ultimate
                        decision,
Deciding upon what is seen or remembered,
Hearing a sound far from any human,
Deciding upon what is real or human,
And they used the white fur as skin and the black wood as shelter,
Standing upon the dry air,
Using the integers until none were left,
Desperately searching for fragments and remnants,
Accepting the achromatic figure and the empty amount.

NOWHERE SO CLOSE AS THE
CENOZOIC MOON

I

I leveled and lifted the land,
Failing between the sea and the air,
Consumed by the tide and the troposphere,
Insignificant behind the transformation and the period,
Or the cataclysmic bee disguised as the modern sting
Darkens the time between the brine and the breeze,
But I reversed my steps to no avail,
Trying to understand the revolution of Saturn and the evolution of man,
Or failing to reverse the history of pollination,
Moving forward behind the constant space,
Stopping at intervals behind the solitary space,
But I reversed my thoughts for future analysis,
Trying to recognize the formation of man,
Or failing to recognize the difference between darkness and night,
A complete isolation of brightness,
Consumed by the mind and the millennium,
And a leveled period disguised as the cataclysmic drone.

II

I departed for the land and the leveled earth,
Not yet upturned,
Trying to lift the shadow of the sun,
Failing to lift the wing from the sea,
Deciding to stop between the dead and the moon,
But I reversed my plan to no avail,
Asking the host about the exact time between life and death,
Or failing to understand the error,
Moving forward behind the precise space,
Timing the intervals behind the transformation and the period,
But I reversed my words for future analysis,
Trying to recognize the transformation of death,
Or the inevitability to recognize the difference between death and
                            mortality,
A minute disclosure of life,

Consumed by the mind and the millennium,
And a leveled period upturned by man on Earth.

IF THE HAND COULD BE SEEN BEFORE THE FACE

They pointed out the tangible thing,
Reminding me of its vast location,
Lost by its omnipresence,
Leaving me to its borrowed time,
Trying to stay on the reversal or the repetition,
But I saw my reflection in the stone,
Or the dark water flowing below Halley's comet
As they pointed out my reflection with averted vision,
Leaving me to its empty glare,
Or leaving me without the peripheral vision,
But when the location can be found,
The size and the shape become unattainable,
Lost by its conclusion,
A distinct possibility of sensory perception,
A magnification of anything unobservable,
And they pointed out to me the vastness of simplicity
And the plainness of complexity,
The entire reason for its sole conclusion,
But I pointed out the stone's reflection,
Or the black leopards running below Neptune's rings
As the philosophers search for the criterion between palm and pupil,
Leaving me among the empty setting,
Past the crowded spot or the open cluster,
A reversal of the repetition
As they pointed out my conception and the mesopic vision.

THE CREATURE BETWEEN DIRT AND DEATH

I

Humans acting like the rain,
And I was dry between drops,
Frustrated between pile and bump,
Estimating a turn from the narrow hole,
Or an animal biting at a frozen heel.

II

The philosophy is too far to be a gene
And too far to inherit,
Or I tried to sing like a tree,
Isolated from the plums and the reason,
Cornered by the space and the mask,
Separated by the music and the bud,
Or I witnessed the veil.

III

The white peak on one side
And the stench of life on the other,
Or the red roses below a dead star,
And the strange people comfortable on the side of the world,
But I only saw the dead roses below the primate's eye.

IV

Energy wasted between the hole and the mind,
A complete segregation of body and thought,
A beginning of the intricate process,
A whole living thing preoccupied with my life,
And I feel the pressure from lost beauty and intimate death.

V

Shadow on the white rock,
Or a shadow from the light,
And I pleaded below the star for time and sun,
Or the beast lies cold under heavy light and a rotation of soil,
A growth process of hair or grass,
A premature thought of a tangible end.

VI

Listen to the space storm,
Light-years from the burial,
A silence above all living things,
A sound billions of years ago,
Like a muffled cry under the frozen sea,
Or the philosophical plane that I searched for without a remainder.

VII

They noticed the human mimicking the wall,
A grotesque impersonation of birth and sleep,
A constant movement of lids and limbs,
A weak force compared to the clouds,
But I noticed the troubled interpretations of death,
A thin layer of earth,
And the clouded birthing.

VIII

Something moving on the space left by Earth,
Or I awoke pressed against the designated spot,
Helpless between oblivion and coherence,
Moving straight toward the mathematical sign,
A sign dug into the earth,
An image naturally planned.

IX

A flock presumed dead by a warm summer day,
And the lonely voice startled by the empty sky,
And I reached for the fading sound,
An intermittent cry,
Identical to mine,
Or similar to dust.

X

Yellow petals invisible on the premature shade,
And the clear water that I brought did not matter,
Since the ocean was already here,
And the yellow petals that I saved died from the invisible flood.

XI

They formed some opinions of the humans and the dead,
But I contradicted some statements
Between the millennium and the mind,
A formal contradiction
Between life and death,
A formal opinion from the humans living
Between time and thought.

XII

I questioned the lack of response,
The total disintegration of beasts and vegetables,
The distance from the moon and the twilight,
Or the total deception of time and thought,
A life span for inevitability and possibility,
The whole period active under dirt and glare.

XIII

The gray side of the shore reflected the gray sand,
And I watched the east before dawn,
Anxious about the movement of light,

Nervous about the stillness of life,
Concerned about the extinction of rocks and stars.

XIV

Humans acting different from the past,
Stepping on empty holes under the lunar eclipse,
Or trying to rationalize the existence of life,
But they ignored the rain and the heel,
Or I realized the definition of void and the similarity of life.

XV

A signal from Titan to the tiger's paw,
A vague distinction between distance and time,
A complete isolation of the two,
The relativity of span and unity,
The isolation that I knew behind rings and reeds,
A distinct recollection between Earth and man.

XVI

I was frightened by the subtleness and the inevitability,
Or they were petrified by the wood and the oak,
But the sequence came on time,
And they went unnoticed among the animate minds,
A position facing the last direction.

XVII

A dim constellation over the pale green ocean,
Or a formal ritual orbiting the future world,
An ancient concept of death and dawn,
But I saw dusk below the winter's sun,
A bright misconception.

XVIII

The casteroides stood gnawing unsuccessfully
On the manmade dam,
And I approached the faraway garden,
Remembering the philosophical thoughts or the psychological plans,
Remembering the past or a literal sequence.

XIX

The apple tree fell in the midst of motion and mass,
And the core or the seed
Falls beneath the broken branch,
Or the astronomer buries the lens near the Precambrian soil,
And I saw the remnants of nothing
Buried beneath the moss and the stone.

XX

Minerals cast upon the round plateau,
But I grieved between the orb,
Resting my head upon the starlight,
Feeling the daytime move randomly in vast eras,
Trying to understand the wholeness
Among the severed points or the severed room.

AN ISLAND AT THE TIP OF DAWN

Rolling space beyond human sight,
As the universe exists alone in the primitive mind,
And the future stops on the empty space,
A parallel life of infinitude and dusk,
A natural selection of sand and sun,
The entire thought of human existence
Broken down in microscopic fragments and tentative suns,
But the first setting became incoherent,
Or the original plan becomes a separation,
A definitive lapse of isolation and light,
A wet edge destined for the rim of land and night,
Or space rolling between the two times the patriofelis lived and the
aardwolf died.

A COUNTLESS LIFE AMONG
THE BEAUTIFUL AIR

A voice from a mind
Thinking of everything below the gray sky,
Speaking to the stars and the rain,
Thinking of humans and crustaceans,
Memorizing the future and the guests,
Forgetting the mind and the sky,
Worried about the black and white void,
But this voice becomes vast and mute,
It becomes a repetition of the past,
A subjectivity for the future,
And the guests voice their opinion for the future,
An exact number of sounds seeking its own level,
Seen by the intruders as philosophy or death,
A whole new occurrence shaping the sequence of life,
Altering the sound of the voice,
Offering the guests a limited space,
Or the budding of a mind thinking about death and philosophy,
A cognitive outcast surrounded by brain waves and burnt excrement,
A number more than zero of everything among the short atmosphere,
And the play continued everywhere beyond reason or its natural limit.

GANYMEDE IS SEEN BY NO ONE
THROUGH THE HIDDEN FENCE

A figure from the Paleocene world
Might have seen the dark shape thinking
Below the massive leaf,
An absence of detail and description,
Or the psychological cat, enormous or growling,
Waiting at the aperture,
And I stood steadfast at the opening,
Waiting for the transformation of moon or star,
And the telescopic eye missed the phase and the human,
Fixing an omniscient mind on nothingness,
Thinking above the small hole,
But I moved along with something bright and alone,
A hidden force lost by time and thought,
A perfect sphere of dents and holes,
A perfect likeness of vacuity or proximity,
The end of a telescopic hole,
But I made the discovery of something already bright and alone,
Something already covered by the transparent sky,
Or the psychological interpretation of metaphysics and the buried scope,
A question constructed from animate parts,
An assemblage without detail and description,
A meeting of the minds without proof or comparatives,
Only the lunar system and the buried post,
But I inquired about myself or the human error,
An arduous guess with fallibility or futility,
A probable aperture without any possible distance.

A PLEA FOR CORDELIA TO THE HANGMAN

Let me express myself beyond the sun's light,
Beyond the warm orange hue,
On bended knees and upturned head,
Wary of void and ghost,
Reaching for the center between the bent height
And the overturned soil,
Holding on below the comet's dust to rope or reason.
And I introduced myself after the late expression,
An expression of emptiness and regret,
A silent appeal between the hemp and the hand,
Or let me gaze at her beauty,
Her tearful eyes and impassive lips,
Or her heart beating loudly through pallid skin,
A similarity between life and death,
Or a contradiction between innocence and experience.
And I reflected on emptiness and regret,
An emptiness beyond the hidden light,
Beyond the finite Earth and the infinite space,
Beyond a human's madness or blindness,
A circular trek behind egg and man,
And the dark glare twinkling below the morning light,
Or the executioner, in a seventeenth-century setting,
Condemning rocks and clouds,
Or let me gaze at her configuration,
Her ring of light and unblemished heart,
Or a similarity between the sun and the star.
And I tried to follow the meaning of life and death,
Or a contradiction between rocks and clouds,
But not one would take heed to my plea,
No one would let me express myself
And compare innocence and experience.

TO COVET THE HEAVENS OR THE INFINITE MIND

It did not mean anything to sit upon the earth
And think about life and death,
Or where I fall, I will lie,
An inevitable reaction between life and death,
A metamorphic reaction with life, air, and earth,
An omniscient mind of emptiness and knowledge,
Or an omnipresent sky of holes and stars,
A dim eye behind a dense view,
Or where I exist, I will die,
An inevitable choice between air and dust,
A natural response with life,
A complete process with the universe,
A vague recollection with time,
But the whole concept was absurd to me and not to the beast,
And it was clear to me that the beast had no conception of this absurdity,
But there was a vague and complete clarity to all this absurdity,
The inevitability of death,
Or where I die, I will not exist,
Or to covet the matter and the infinite space.

THE RAVEN AND THE SNOW

The contrast would become gray
In comparison to brain and thought,
And I sat under the gray tree
Thinking about the wings and the water,
And I decided to remember the caw and the cold,
An uncanny sight for a telescopic view,
So close to see the land and the sea,
And I decided to learn about the black and white setting,
Or a gray horizon frozen below the avian night,
And I could hear the subtle drift,
Black as the crow's eye or white as the winter's rain,
But when the heat formed behind the southern plains,
The contrast would become gray in comparison to feather and flake,
And I sat reading the poems thinking about life and death,
Reading about the white walls or the black ceiling and floors,
But this all appeared in the unconscious,
The heavens and Earth, the whiteness, the black bird, the frosted hills,
So I studied the consciousness of living things,
Or the daytime sleep of human beings,
An identical poem of white trees melting below the sable flock,
The comparison was different from anything in the conscious mind,
So I studied the contrast of life or the certainty of human death,
An identical shape of visibility melting below the avian void,
But time was lost to us,
And it snowed tomorrow upon the white earth,
And the frozen white bird.... dead.

MY HEART BEATS NEXT TO THE SUN

I

Time has come upon the distant rays,
And the measured turn forms below the ultimate guise,
And the orange face follows the earthly matter,
A miscalculation on the fourth state of matter,
But I thought about reality through a shaded eye,
Or a permanent screen placed between tomorrow and the past,
And the measured light forms a miscalculation on the earthly life,
But I thought it will be a permanent state,
A bright day below the astronomical state,
A subtle appearance without warning,
A preoccupation for humans,
Or my preoccupation on human thought,
The same as the span of life,
And my conversation between myself and the soil,
A human pattern philosophizing between Earth and sun,
An earthly process that I must ponder or accept,
A strange sensitivity to the light,
And the same as the beating heart.

II

Space has come between the distant rays,
And I turned below the cloudy skies,
Or the heat settled below the grizzled setting,
And the orange face rose from peak and dwelling,
A miscalculation on the human race,
But I thought about everyday life through a shaded sun,
An optical screen between the past and the sun,
And the measured life forms a miscalculation on the earthly light,
But I thought about myself among the astronomical state,
A measurable entity like a celestial being,
A preoccupation for the future,
Or my preoccupation on human history,
The same as the span of the atmosphere and the chromosphere,
And my conversation on the brevity of life,
A sound philosophizing between myself and a human being,

A final process that I must ponder or accept,
A strange sensitivity to life,
And the same as the beating light.

THE PHILOSOPHER'S GUIDE
TO AN IMPERFECT WORLD

I. The Wall

You gave your attention to the laughter
That dissipated behind the cognitive mind,
And I waited the entire age for the incorrect answer,
Leaning my entire weight on the vertical soil,
Witnessing the laughter behind the bright aperture,
And you gave your insight to the sphere
That moved beyond the vast periphery,
And I held out my entire weight for the gravitational pull,
Witnessing the tears behind the concave soil,
And you gave your probability to the brontotherium
That evolved around the microscopic circle,
And I waited briefly at the hole,
Leaning my entire breath on the vertical rim,
Filling it with dusk and air,
Trying to separate laughter and tears,
But you remained breathing under the minute hand,
Watching me observe the bright enclosure and the improper fraction,
Watching a grotesque spot instead of the hole.

II. The Cave

You gave your attention to the precipitation
That continued before the tearful eyes,
And I lifted the side of this circular equation,
Expecting to see a primate or the results,
Anticipating the darkness at the end of the light,
And you gave your response to the angle of the sun
That made a fraction of the day,
And I guessed at the difference between the star and the moon,
Figuring the longevity of a horizontal being,
And you stalled because of the limited time
That occurred only to the superior mind,
A destiny that became a challenge for the two species
Between the oceans and the rain,

And I stood near the arid land,
Lifted by the circular sand,
Trying to separate thoughts and words,
But your thoughts were put into words,
Thoughts and words conveyed to flowers, reptiles, and fish,
Watching me observe the eggs and the bees,
Watching the color of the waters instead of the sky.

III. The Stone

You gave your attention to the enormous haze
That settled upon the upturned palm,
And I counted the lines in the earth,
Ready to subtract after the modern era,
Willing to read about the final point,
And you gave the dirt to the sea,
A transformation from mud to dirt,
And I began to feel the similarity in time,
A constant formation of insolubility and ideologies,
Or an illusive reminder of the solvent and the plan,
But you divided the texture according to the enormity of thought,
A small length of time given to the swarm and the herd,
But I reached the bottom of the surface,
Stranded against the blue sky,
Repeating the conversation to the spot of light,
Holding the vapor with one finger against the blue surface,
And you settled upon the time span,
Indented from the silence and the species,
Perpetrated by the sound and the simplicity,
A remembrance orchestrated by you during the time span,
An equivalent conversation to the same species as the original form,
But as a complex question.

IV. The Cliff

You gave your attention to the woeful snake
That curled around the visible air,
And I mentioned the question, again, under the crooked limb,
Under the overripe fruit,
Witnessing the height of the inanimate ground,

And you gave your opinion of the dense aroma
That moved below the water's edge,
And I held out my hand just before the total eclipse,
Hoping to hear the geological formation,
Hoping to see the error or the sand,
But when the light fell upon the ledge,
The borhyaena staggered gracefully upon the toppled soil,
And the vegetation covered the empty foundation,
Bringing the laughter closer to the great sphere,
But you remained skeptical or convinced about the entire weight,
A partial answer to the original plan,
A time span for the modern era,
Void of the spot or the complexity,
And I remained unconvinced about the entire age,
Or the whole process of excavation, perfection, and cognition,
An entire hole filled with time.

THE GENETICS OF A PHILOSOPHER'S HOUND

I listened carefully to the conversation
About the existence of God,
I listened on Earth's surface,
Or I heard the conversation between two animate objects,
Between human beings between the sea and the tree,
Or we asked the impossible between the conversation and the earth,
But I heard the ending from a distance,
The beginning as we know it,
But I interrupted the conversation with a profound question
Or an incorrect answer,
And we listened to the anthropologist and the astronomer,
And I listened to the roots and the waves,
An inaudible conversation between one animate object,
The whole concept of God and man buried under the air,
Exhumed from the mind,
Altered by time and place,
So I put my ear to Earth's surface,
Or I heard the shifting of the plates,
The shifting between Earth and mind,
A solitary planet and a single thought,
A vast loneliness between question and answer,
But I remained between dry shore and dead leaves,
Or the two inanimate objects,
But we walked carefully toward the agreement,
An indefinite conclusion between two human beings,
A finality between the wall and the cliff.

THE SILENT BELLS FROM CALLISTO

I saw Earth from a great distance,
From a microscope,
From an eyepiece pressed hard against the atmosphere,
From all life that ceased to exist,
From the birth of an invisible life,
And from the ancient stars
The light began to exist,
Or nothingness ended before the light ceased to exist,
And I saw Earth for the first time behind the great sphere,
Behind years or sunsets,
But civilization obtained the telescope,
Learning to focus on mind and space,
Or learning to adjust the lens between birth and death,
And I realized the insignificance or the severity of life,
The beauty under the slide,
Under the sky,
Under the entire mind,
Behind the entire space,
And I looked on the brighter side and heard the unseen sounds,
Or the dark gray bird perched on the small red spot,
And the direction changed its meaning from the past to the future,
Changing the direction of thought and meaning,
A thought process changed only by space or the future,
A finite reminder for humans conscious of memory and meaning,
Conscious of the microscopic Earth,
And I saw myself for the first time,
Old and invisible,
Mortal and visible,
A spectacle against the lens,
A human being amongst the void,
Or a speck against the ancient stars,
And I saw myself alive against dead minds,
Solitary confinement,
Naked beings,
The whole world against the sky,
The whole sound mute against myself.

THE HOLE AND THE LIGHT

Civilization beckoned society from the dark hills,
And the dogs ran scared in both directions from the last decision,
Or I remained here according to the logic,
Immobile and free according to the last decision,
And wolves and coyotes played dead or fetched sticks
Under the perforated sun,
And the whole cognitive process faded piecemeal after rocks and reptiles,
A human process piecemeal before the bright abyss,
And civilization started life behind the high peaks,
A race from the dawn to the flash,
A society unsettled between dawn and civilization,
Or I went there according to the cognitive process,
Unwilling to separate logic from inevitability,
A race according to civilization,
But the fire and the rain faded piecemeal behind the dark hills,
And some processed their thoughts,
Or remained there according to logic.

MORE ROSES THAN DIRT

An impossibility reached the closest point of infinity,
So I estimated the last thought with measurements and life,
A proposed theory for humus and thorns,
Or the scent of petals and earth,
A possible convergence of fourteen billion years,
An absolute mortality of the closest point,
But I reached the end of the closest garden,
Or the closest end of the garden,
The immediate point in life,
The farthest end of the flowerpot,
And I was alone at the end,
Waiting for dust to become earth,
Waiting for the petals to become life,
Waiting for the first formation of time, numbers, and ideas,
But the human fear grew like infinite space from the ground and the mind,
It battled two constant thoughts of the inevitability and the unknown,
An unconscious war and peace with mind and time,
Or a mathematical variation of measurements and ground,
But I reached the end of the closest point,
Tripping over the farthest end or stepping over the freshly dead,
A permanent display of infinity or a temporary stay of death.

THE UNIVERSE IS SO SMALL
COMPARED TO THE INSIDE

What thoughts formulate in the minds of human beings?
What instincts formulate in the minds of the predator and the prey?
What have the stars to do with a solitary life?
And I compared my instincts to my thoughts,
Or the room to nothingness,
And the ceiling to the soil,
A future comparison to the wall and the light,
Or the stars and the darkness,
And I compared all human thoughts to all human instincts,
An instinctive guess to my own thoughts,
A possible probability to ceiling and prey,
And I compared my own thoughts to the inside,
An unequal transmission from room to room,
A universal balance of insignificance and conveyance,
A human instinct for significance and possibility,
A mind so small compared to the outside,
Or the room to vastness,
The formulation of circles and emptiness,
And I compared the universe to all human beings,
Including myself and the ultimate finality,
Or I observed and compared the inside to the first light and the last
darkness.

SOUNDS BEYOND THE SILENT TONGUE
A POEM IN ONE ACT

GOD: Wouldst thou hunt between the beginning and dawn, and move with life under the heavens, extending thy range of original birth or flourish Earth with subtle domain, created in the time before man, living on growth and birth, sharing this land, existing on Earth in peace and plentitude with thyself and thy kind. But throughout the time thine use is for procreation and flesh by beast and slaughter and profit by man, but thou art here in this place without reproach or sin.

BEAST: Thy name I know, an ultimate force of omniscience and all that exists, the unending sign of space and light, an existence immeasurable from the first seed of life, or the birth from the beginning of the void, thy name be above all that ever lived, a name revered by the heavenly light, even the darkness concedes to thine omnipotence. But I ask thee, from the beginning among the mystery of the garden and the future society, is it the sin of man or beast?

GOD: Yea, 'tis the sin of man unto Earth and unto himself. I hath given him power over all on Earth, a role that time hath proven the serpent's friend, from all the days of nakedness to waters under the sun. What lesson will learn this cognitive mind? A lesson to forsake all his power, an Earth of soil and sky, an Earth of flora and fauna.

BEAST: But am I guilty of the sin, the one who prowls before sun and man, the form that moves with shadow and moon, a creation that takes its shape in sea, land, and sky, a vast observer of life, a quiet observer of death, a provider of flesh for man and other beasts, the flesh and milk that sustains and drains life? But I long sensed the foul air, a constant cause of fear and dread, not the kind from fog or glare, but from an observation of man's existence.

GOD: Thou art not of shame, 'tis the tiller and the keeper in which man exits and begets his kind below the stars, a stain upon sky and Earth.

BEAST: I feel all the fauna as my kind. I feel us all as one as the sun and the moon will rotate their light and darkness, and I feel the flora in my domain, but 'tis man I fear as my greatest enemy.

GOD: Here is thy place on Earth with thy kind and all that exits under the heavens, feast well and multiply, let thine instincts roam this Earth, and let the flora and the fauna satisfy thy needs.

BEAST: Days were good in the beginning with the creation of light, and the darkness filled with the creation of all the luminous spheres and the grasses covered Earth's land, nourished by the waters from the great mist. But then came a change in time with dust and breath, an image of flesh and bone, a keeper of light and dark.

GOD: Thou question my creation of man and seek answers to my image?

BEAST: Nay, I fear for all the flora and all of my kind. We use the finite Earth to survive and multiply. But man hath altered that finitude, stripping Earth for his own kind.

GOD: 'Tis true, by all the light in the heavens and on Earth, and by all the creation from the beginning unto the end.

BEAST: 'Tis my existence, under the solar and the lunar eclipse, and by all the universe from the reign of man unto the void, 'tis my fate.

DEATH AT THE FOUR CORNERS OF EARTH

Behold the brevity of life,
And the quick observation of stars and birth,
Or behold the galaxy and the empty egg,
Or I turned the telescope at eye level,
Reaching the ground and the atmosphere,
Searching for the curves and the end,
Blocked by the clarity and the glare,
Deceived by the land and the air,
But I turned my eye to the beginning,
To the space between Earth and sky,
Miscalculating the irregular womb and the spiral death,
Or the eyepiece was cut by three-fourths,
And the navigation of humans continued through the dense fog,
Through the waves and wind,
Over the swells and clouds,
Beneath the night and the black sun,
Or I turned a mirror toward the corner of the room,
Waiting to see the image of death and humans,
Waiting to see the extent of life,
But I was kept waiting for an indefinite time,
Kept waiting under the same corner and curve,
The same image as the day and the sun,
The exact image of life.

THE COMPLETE EXPERIMENTATION
FROM BACTERIAL SIGNS TO BIOGENIC MINDS

They dissolved their differences
Between human beings and signs,
And they reached the pinnacle of the sea and the abyss of the mind,
Or I took my complaints to the fossils, the apes, and the sun,
But the difference will be between the signs and the mind,
Or I approached the ideas at the lowest level,
Well aware of the psychological transformation
And the cognitive pandemic,
An absolute obscurity from beginning to end,
The open experiment from garden to sea,
Or the documented time from soil to sand,
But I took leave of my ground
And approached the spot at the highest level,
Seeking the information or the answer to the results of the time line,
A process or progression,
Well aware of human beings and the lowest level of existence,
But I stayed near the rocks,
Convinced of the experiment between the garden and the sea,
A process of elimination between human beings and the lowest level of
existence.

INTELLIGENT LIFE?

I

I reasoned with the humans to no avail,
Or I cited the great pyramids and the space exploration,
Or I convinced the brown dog of my sincerity,
Lying down below the rain and the sun,
Sculpting a configuration among inanimate objects and brain density,
But I reasoned with myself in the reflection and in my mind,
Eliminating the senses for cognition or the natural instinct,
Behaving like the modern species below the yellow clouds,
Familiar with the transition or the level of advancement
Between the dirt and the white petal,
And I rationalized the illogical state,
A definite matter of theory and existence,
A natural course of events with probability and end,
A definite conclusion with opinions or originality,
And I spoke logically to the brown and yellow bird,
Hoping for a coherent response.

II

I reasoned with the plants on a different level,
Or I was standing below the rain and the sun on a lower plateau,
Or I convinced the brown dog of my imperfection,
Measuring the distance between the instinct and the scheme,
Relying on the space between the object and the density,
But I reasoned with myself between the gate and the fence,
Establishing the senses for cognition or natural instinct,
Behaving like the modern species in the ancient world,
Familiar with the night and the day or the height of advancement
Between the input and the outcome,
And I rationalized the logical state,
A matter of theory and existence,
A course of events with a possibility and an end,
A conclusion with opinions or originality,
And I spoke logically to the white petal,
Hoping for a response.

EVOLUTION OF THE VOID

I noticed the physicist behind the gravedigger,
And the light from the womb became a light-year,
And the proximity of life became a memory,
And the light from the star became a dream,
But I noticed the progression suddenly pause, reverse, then accelerate,
A constant motion detected by life or a certain species undetected by
time,
And the proximity of time became a reality,
Or I stopped and withdrew into view,
A palpable progression from memory and evolution,
Identical from human to death,
And the whole existence became a vacuum of genes capable of birth,
Lasting for an unknown period of time,
Lasting between the science and the soil,
Ending between the sea and the soil,
Or the fish and the tree became evidence for life,
And I sat between the void and the mass,
Nothing more than wet leaves and the time it took humans to remember
The hot bright sun and the cold dark Earth,
Or the time between the past and the future.

THE TWILIGHT BETWEEN DUSK AND LIGHT

I

I could see the difference on the stone,
Or the impossibility invisible to the eye,
But the relationship of human and Earth
Lasted for a tentative time,
It remained visible for a time on Earth and stone.

II

The view was blocked by nothingness and minds,
And the sight was justified by flowers and the dead,
And the waiting was justified by the birth and the buds,
Or they organized thoughts from beginning to end,
From an unknown setting between the ground and the sky.

III

They confronted me on Earth about time and space,
Or the people lived on Earth between the rocks and the seas,
A sociological transformation from sun to new moon,
Or a dim glow from past to progression,
And a dead petal on the rocks and the seas.

IV

I viewed the difference between nothingness and the mind,
And it was justified by the light on Earth,
An external feature between the mind and the past,
Or I remembered the variation of life and extent of death.

V

Matter and mind from the beginning,
And thought or process in the midst of human existence,
And I felt isolated without a reason,
Without a guarantee of the yellow sun and the process of thought.

VI

But the whole concept of loneliness or life
Became a mixture among the sociological air,
And I felt that concept and divided that mixture,
Pondering upon the elements of life,
Dealing with the idea of the dead,
And the whole process of being.

VII

I sensed a similarity in life and death,
And I reached the point of observation or certain depth,
And I sensed the trees swaying and the rocks forming,
Or the complexity between the mind and the outside world.

VIII

The probability of life exceeding death
Became a fantasy between the mind and the external stimuli,
And the reality of death exceeding life
Became an inevitability,
Where the sea meets the air and the earth meets the grass.

IX

A white bird flew over the swollen womb,
But the sky was filled with haze and light,
Or I stopped beneath the bright gray air
Listening for the celestial voice,
But the thunder became a reality,
A universal sound for all living things.

X

And the depth of logic ran parallel to the finitude of life,
Or the massive wind rested on the yellow flower,
And the limited sun rested on the red petal,
But I viewed the difference between being and the mind,
And it was perceived by existence.

XI

A great fault ran between earth and the human mind,
And the rain covered the wet plateau,
Or I sensed the difference between nothingness and death,
And a great fault ran between omnipresence and extinction,
Unlike the color and the light.

XII

I walked on the vagueness of Earth and axis,
A space below nadir or wing,
A crag below the sky and the dead,
Or the black leopard slept before the white mist,
And I stopped below the beautiful trees,
A space below pinnacle or sole.

XIII

The orange tree remained visible for a time on Earth,
And the people lived for a time between the ground and the rinds,
And the color became lost between the yellow and the red,
But I saw the miacis near the civets
Lapping up the invisible juice.

XIV

A philosophy book made of excrement and light
Perished under the rose-colored bough,
And the burial smelled of grapevines,
Or life exceeded the geometric garden,
And I arrived too late for the leveled soil,
A corner from a rectangular hole.

XV

I heard small laughter under the cloud bank,
A child asleep under the white pollen
Dreaming of dragons and life,
Dreaming of fantasy and death,

But I heard the fire and the fear,
A distant tree or a nervous sigh,
An unconscious reality.

XVI

I sat fully aware of the sun and the sea,
But frightened of time and tide,
In oblivion and proximity of cosmic rays and death,
Or I sat directly on Earth's surface,
Weeping at the wet dirt and the daytime star.

XVII

Clouds and moons were points of white against the human eye.
And the heavy days began under the white sky,
Or time became a fossil and a dream,
An unconscious mind of theories and uncertainty,
A clear vision of mist and Earth.

XVIII

The reptile moved from snow to sand or from shade to light,
And I listened to the dialogue between civilization and extinction,
An inaudible exchange between two people,
Or a vociferous play staged on the rocks of Ceres.

XIX

I remembered the dead lawn and the grassland,
But I had forgotten the thylacosmilus and the cyperaceae,
But I remembered the orange leaves and the melancholy poems,
And the comparison between mammals and roots,
Or the contrast in humans and civilization.

XX

The bells approached the most recent times
Where the sound emulates the vast isolation
And silence beckons the last tree,

Or the articulation ceased below the first sky,
And the natural road became part of death,
Or omnipotence in weeds and dust.

ONCE UPON A TIME IN THE DISTANT FUTURE

I gave myself pause for the stoic observation
Between cognition and landscape,
And I dreamt under the sun of brain matter and horrific scenery,
But the okapi walked quietly under the yellow sun,
And the solitary bee will be hovering over the deep bright hole,
Or humans gathered in the corner,
Discussing the possibility of life and death
Or the infinite space,
Deciding the distance between the past and the future,
And I gave myself room to reflect
On the corner and the space,
A decision about humans and death,
A countless number of thoughts between Earth's flowers and Jupiter's
                                    moons,
The solitary thought of isolation and life,
A view of closeness or tears,
The longevity of dawn falling down behind the midnight slumber,
And I gave myself nothing
Compared to the nonexistence and the universe,
Or a human thought about a quince tree growing on Charon,
The solitary conception from generation to generation,
The absolute misconception from time or birth.

WHERE ON EARTH ARE THE COGNITIVE SIGNS?

The same response differs from conversation and communication,
And I became quite tired from all the matter,
From all the gray signs behind the laughter,
Or I struggled with the possibility of an inevitable death,
And a conscious decision of a terminal life,
But the children and the dogs remained behind the laughter,
Initiating the signs of dreams and unconsciousness,
Initiating the hidden interpretation,
Reconstructing the molecular signs behind grayness and matter,
Or I struggled with the inevitability of a possible death,
And an unconscious decision of a terminal life,
But the communication became extinct,
And I realized the reflection of the mirror and the eclipse,
Or I realized the direction of humans and the total matter,
A precise alienation of intellect and civility,
Or the oceans and the sky between thinking skills and legible dirt,
And I became part of the total destruction,
An unwilling participant between conversation and death,
A new examination of Earth, flat and bare,
Or the beautiful garden of rinds and skin behind the wasteland.

I SUFFERED THE EFFECTS OF ISOLATION AND OMNIPRESENCE

I

ISOLATION

I heard the dense population in mind and body,
And my eyes level with space and time,
Or the infinite length between petal and stem,
Or I listened to the crowd between black and white,
Like a sea of gray rolling in chaos and contemplation,
An immediate cause of mass confinement,
Or I listened to the lull between multitude and being,
Like a swarm of locusts on Deimos,
An immediate pause of existence.

II

OMNIPRESENCE

I heard the vast emptiness in space and time,
And my eyes level with mind and body,
Or the finite length between sun and light,
Or I listened to the cry between the twilight air,
Like a sea of clouds rolling in soil and sleep,
An immediate cause of mass hysteria,
Or I listened to the sound between vision and perception,
Like a solitary beast on Earth,
An immediate source of extinction.

I WITNESSED THE EFFECTS OF BIRTH AND DEATH

I knew the reality as thought and being,
Or anything that existed between life,
And the final breath from womb or space,
A definition of proof for unconsciousness and observation,
Or a delicate layer of earth and an infinite sky,
But I wandered into the bright setting,
Knowing full-well of its dark surrounding,
Or the yellow setting reflecting the dead beings,
But I calculated reality as proof of life,
A reflection as thought and time,
A whole different conception between the seed and the sleep,
An immeasurable length of time between womb and space,
And the green grass stopped growing,
And Saturn stopped turning on its axis,
Or I became caught between metaphysics and human life,
A transition between thoughts and action,
A philosophical being among the universe,
The questions remained unanswered,
Or I stopped behind the enormous stone
Waiting for the prograde motion of Venus
And the tall grass to bend in the gentle breeze,
But the light became brighter on the great rock.

THE ONTOLOGICAL GUEST

I came closer,
But they spoke louder about death, God, and void,
And I felt such a great distance from life, universe, and matter,
Or I became present from the absence of time,
An absolute stranger from my host,
As a white flower on Pluto or a dead dog on Mars,
But I became an invitation,
Born after the void and during the matter,
Trying to learn about life and death,
Trying to learn how to live with my host,
Struggling to survive between the entrance and the exit,
Trying to maintain a delicate balance between the sound and the silence,
Trying to understand everything between the host and the guest,
But I thought about the dead tree between distance and time,
So I reasoned with my existence or my reflection in the bark,
Learning how I could never overstay my welcome or make this my
                    permanent home.

EUROPA IN THE FAR CORNER
OF A GEOCENTRIC VOID

From surface to atmosphere or land to gas,
Humans continue in tangible thought or ideological form,
Or apes huddle under the full moon,
Comparing brain matter with people and genealogy,
Comparing the dirt with the blue sky,
And I compared dirt with rain,
And I knew the contrast of stone and snow,
But when people acknowledged themselves as human,
I compared day with light,
A complete process of elimination with black and white,
Or a grayness settling quietly on noise and chaos,
A subtle elimination of progression and pause,
A sudden growth of position and past,
But I followed the comparison and contrast of humans and Earth,
The self-realization of people and myself,
The horrific void of chaos and noise,
The arduous stop between reason and remembrance,
The vague gesture of humans to stop and think,
A lost reference of apes mimicking under the crescent Earth,
And I knew the uncertainty in a lull or limbo,
A certainty in progression or future uncertainty,
The ingredients in the subconscious of nature,
Or the genetic make-up of the consciousness of man,
A realistic view from myself and the dirt-covered wall,
A vivid imagination of reality and history,
Or the last person thinking among the dense atmosphere
As an old person surviving on the surface,
Thinking among the entire length of day and light.

HUMANS BEHIND THE SMALL THOUGHTS
AND THE GRAY AIR

We sat in the dark facing the sun
With our backs to the night,
Or they asked me about the riddle in the pale white sunlight,
And my reflection began to weep
As I carried the damp light from monkey to magnification,
And the people began to argue about the difference between the two,
An argument classified by astronomers and paleoanthropologists,
And we stood in the light facing the ground,
But I managed to walk upright through isolation and life,
A limited capacity for infinite thoughts and colorless air.

THEY SENSED THE SHEPHERD
BURYING A TRILLION SHEEP

And they buried them under the wall,
Under the moonlight,
Under the red stars,
And I overturned the light and the soil in order to survive,
Or the green hills were altered by the sunlight,
And they waited here under the wool,
As the wolves patrolled the distant hills,
Circling the grassy peaks,
Stopping to defecate on the small hole,
Or they waited here under the waste,
But the bell sounded to distract the real meaning,
It was sensed by the entire flock
And dismissed by the entire pack,
A complete generation standing in line between the seaweed and the sand,
Torn between the conception of the waste and the grassy peak,
And I read about the complete generation
While I stood between the light and the soil,
Or it became everyone's guess as to the identity of Earth or death,
So I slowly walked past the fossil of a dire wolf
Or desperate to see if there was any evidence of light under the wall,
Any trace of human evolution or an anthropomorphic creation.

THE PHILOSOPHER'S MAP TO THE PHILISTINE'S LAIR

The results were far from over,
Almost a parsec according to the human mind,
Almost a measurement of time,
Almost a totality for the formula or directions,
And I was caught among the air and the weight
Or the crust and the mantle,
But the erosion left out the tracks,
So I spent the time among measurements and ideas,
Listening to the sound of the wind and the dens,
Deciphering the difference between limestone and slate,
Or they had a vision of Aristotle walking with a compass and cane,
But the erosion left out the vertical prints,
A sporadic reminder of wisdom or barbarity,
And the whole test was inaccurate because of distance and location,
Or they performed an accurate test because of the Modern Age,
And I realized the seriousness of the compass and the cane,
Whether it be Plato or Socrates,
But the sight of the wind changed because of its hue,
It changed direction below the atmosphere,
Flowing above the land,
Shaking the sign and the sky,
Meeting the course toward a conscious setting,
Or they had the same vision of a crowded den,
But the results were far from an exact location.

EVEN THE WEEPING COULD NOT BE HEARD ON CERES

I

It remained aloof in front of the invisible reeds,
A great distance between the tangible stalks and the hollow seeds,
And the request was stifled,
Conveyed by sound,
Heard by the gases and the rocks,
A dim echo dismissed by the imagination,
Eliminated by the proof of existence,
But the mild night changed from black to white,
And from the mild blue sky began the salty rain,
A dry mixture between land and air,
An infinite statement of something never to have been known
Or never to have lived.

II

They stopped in front of the bent grass,
But it looked more like a tangible ghost and a hollow reed,
And the request was postponed until further notice,
Conveyed by voice,
Heard by the dying and the dead,
A dull vision dismissed by an explanation,
Liquidated by the finality of life,
But the dark side changed from black to white,
And from the calm white sky began the salty rain,
A dense mixture between land and air,
An infinite statement of something never to have been understood
Or never to have survived.

III

I wept upon the deaf ears and the blind eyes,
Or I shouted from the spot,
Light-years from the world,
And my request was categorized with extinction and nothingness,
But the morning sun was in guise as the dawn,

Or the thunder clouds rained upon the salty earth,
Taking the place of the screams and the tears,
But the morning sun blocked the spot of light from the new world,
So I corresponded with the mute and introduced myself to the dead stars,
A great distance between tangible ghosts and invisible reeds.

OH, SEE THE OLIVE TREES SWAYING
IN THE VOID

Empty hands holding on to the twigs and the capillaries,
Sweaty palms clenching the cognitive mind,
And the stems smelled of skunk,
And the sea smelled of stars,
But the air was still and odorless,
Or civilization gathered amid hurricane and fragrance,
But the air was in the cognitive mind,
A process or plan for humans to create and destroy,
A process of elimination for ideas and individuality,
But I witnessed space in the void,
An empty palm holding the heart and the roots,
Or the dark sun shining below the blinding light,
And the empty space filled with cognitive void,
A vacillation between humans and civilization,
A complete metamorphosis of bark and fruit,
But I witnessed time in the empty space,
A natural possibility in a probable world,
Or a beautiful occurrence behind the ugliness and the blinding light,
A sight altered by stability.

THE PORPOISE THAT WAS BURIED ON LAND

I prepared for the elevation,
A subterranean level below the clouds and the fog,
Below the voices and the clarity,
But I remembered the past,
The selected few absorbed in the countless mass,
A vast resurrection of fish and birds,
But they forgot the level,
A dense sight between ledge and altitude,
But I suggested mammalogy or the burial at sea,
And the fog became the clouds,
And the clouds at sea level,
And they thought the fish could breathe the air,
Or the grave reached its level with water and birds,
A vast distance between bones and land,
And I sensed the estimation of salt and sediment,
A clear sight between the elevation,
Or a vague thought between dolphins and humans.

THE THING BETWEEN SOIL AND SPACE

I

The dead light floating in the air,
Landing on the horizontal pate,
Moving simultaneously with the time of day,
Moving with the wind and the geographical location,
But the dead air became the atmosphere,
And the great apes inhaled and exhaled below the empty bough.

II

The people that stood in the brightness
Classified themselves as human beings,
They measured the confinements and the open air,
Or they confined themselves to the middle ground,
But the outcome acted like a great force,
A product of the sole inertia.

III

It was compared to the mist moving from top to bottom,
Moving like a great force,
Developing like a human being,
Settling upon the earth and the sky,
Reacting to life and death,
Or settling upon the first bud and the first born.

IV

I arrived on time near the falling space,
Or the beauty on Earth veiled by the falling mist,
A perpetual progression of finitude and death,
A cognitive perception of progression and life,
Or the finitude of life between all humans.

V

And the dogs sniffing at dirt and pate,
Waging their tails at the confinement and the cognition,
Sensing the past and the place,
Barking at the humans and the apes,
But I sensed the future and the pate,
Or the connection between man and ape.

VI

The entity never existed between the core and the exosphere,
But humans believed they existed between thoughts and tangibility,
But I sensed the future between experience or knowledge,
Or the connection between fish and air.

VII

The tiglon walked nervously under the great branch,
Scratching at the rotted bough,
Urinating on the cylindrical leaf,
Or the day compared to the dirt,
A beautiful rose grew bright red,
Dying as a guest under the cold light,
Prostrate under the hound's tail.

VIII

I arrived late near the occupied space,
Or the beauty on Earth clear as the horizontal mist,
A perceptual progression of finitude and life,
A cognitive perception of progression then death,
Or the finitude of life between humans and birth.

IX

And the night alive with darkness and stars,
Or Earth clear as the horizontal light,
Measured by humans and apes,
Extinct by time and Earth,

Replenished by sea and land,
Or the beauty in thoughts clear as the finitude of life,
A measurement of perception and time.

X

The highest mountain level with the plains and the earth,
Or the dogs sniffing at apes and the pate,
Whimpering at the hill or the peak,
But I walked around the light
Waiting for the progression to move with human thought.

XI

DNA behind the sea level or behind the sun's rays,
And the people forming a society from the brine and the brightness,
And the children forming a word from their minds or their experience,
But the hail lifted quickly over the leopard's coat.

XII

It was compared to the myopia moving from right to left,
Moving like a large speck,
Developing like a civilization,
Settling upon the dead and the living,
Reacting to Earth and time,
Or settling upon the base and the water.

XIII

The okapi stood alert under the gray branch,
Yawning at the cylindrical glare,
Urinating on the invisible soil,
Or the day compared to the dirt,
A beautiful rose grew,
Dying as a plant under the cold light,
Erect under the warm hail.

XIV

I arrived between sunrise and the stars,
Or the beauty on Earth changed from perception to void,
A perceptual progression among inevitability and death,
A thought process over the life span of humans,
Or the beauty on Earth changed permanently.

XV

Blood in the universe became a sign of insignificance
Like the brown pile or the yellow stain,
But the children acted like adults on stage,
Creating a role for the seed or the egg,
Treating the infants like humans,
Or playing hide-and-seek with the dirt and the air.

XVI

The road ended near the wall,
So the village built a garden near the road,
A garden behind the wall,
And the village suffered from delusions of grandeur,
Imitating a civilization or a factitious wall,
Believing the open road.

XVII

The simian gesturing in the air,
Landing on the vertical pate,
Moving simultaneously with the time of day,
Moving with the dust and the exact spot,
But I walked around the dead air,
Waiting for the human thought,
Waiting for the vertical tree.

XVIII

It was compared to the fire moving from left to right,
Moving like a tiny star,
Developing like a cold sunrise,
Settling upon the dead and the living,
Reacting to progression,
Or the ape began to barter with humans for light and heat.

XIX

I arrived among the dead,
Sensing the birth and the breath,
Or the beauty on Earth changed from horror to life,
A thought process while conscious,
An unconscious pattern while existing,
But the beauty became subjective,
And the space between became objective.

XX

The entity existed among human thoughts,
But humans believed they existed between the core and the exosphere,
Or they were oblivious between the roots and the stars,
But I sensed the future between the dead light and the empty bough.

THE SERVAL AND THE PHILOSOPHER'S PET

The bright figure looked exactly like the dark shape,
Or the existence before birth and after death,
Or the space between omniscience,
But I searched between collar and leash or neck and hand,
Or I searched behind the white fog,
And the figure took shape,
But the white flower died under the heavy rain
Causing time to be measured or forgotten,
Transforming the hairy neck and the long hands,
But they cast the seed upon the frozen sea or stone and foam,
Or they cast the sand behind the white fog
Causing time to be quantified or neglected,
But I searched between skin and earth,
Or the philosophy could be detected from the mind or the external
                              stimuli,
And the philosophy could be deduced from the petal and the wetness,
But the fauna searched between solid and liquid or behind the white fog,
A pause between the search and the existence,
A continuation behind the last setting,
But I realized the possible space between birth and death.

MOONLIGHT ON BETELGEUSE

I only thought about the difference,
A wasted thought in an empty room,
Or a complicated solution in a perpetual space,
And I am a human being between the solution and the wasted thought,
A parallel existence between isolation and death,
But I asked the wrong question in subjective form,
Or substituting objectivity for conjecture,
But I asked the sleeping child the right question
As Titan moved asymmetrically behind the yellow cloud,
But I asked the howling wolf the right question
As Alpha Centauri stopped periodically below the crescent shape,
Or I received no answer from both questions,
Since the wolf slept near the whining child,
And I thought about the one question
While comparing the tears with the subconscious,
While comparing the blue sky with the green grass,
And I thought about the many questions among the vast population,
A reflection on life between solitude and sunlight.

GRAY MATTER AMONG THE EMPTY GRAIN
A POEM IN ONE ACT

GOD: Wouldst thou rise from the breath and walk with life under the heavens, extending thy range over Earth with superior domain, created in the time after dawn, living on the crust and the dust, sharing this land, existing on Earth in conflict and multitude with thine own kind. But throughout the time thine use is for procreation and harmony and not for slaughter and profit, but thou art here in this place with reproach and sin.

MAN: Thy name I know well, an ultimate force of omniscience and all that exists, the unending sign of space and light, an existence immeasurable from the first seed of life, or the birth from the beginning of the void, thy name be above all that ever lived, a name that is omnipotent and unknown, even in darkness thy name be all that exists in the universe. But I ask thee, from the beginning of the Garden to the end of civilization, is it the sin of man?

GOD: Yea, 'tis thy sin unto Earth. I hath given thee power over all on Earth, a role that time hath proven the serpent's friend, from all the days of nakedness to all of Earth under the sun. What lesson will learn thy cognitive mind? A lesson to forsake all thy power, an Earth of land and water, an Earth of only plants and beasts.

MAN: But am I guilty of the sin, the one who walks among plants and beasts, the image that walks under the sun, a creature that takes its shape from thine own, a cognitive observer of life and death, a provider of existence for plants and beasts, a provider of cognitive progression for humankind?

GOD: Thou art of shame, 'tis Adam and Eve in which thou were begotten, a stain upon sky and Earth.

MAN: I share Earth with all the fauna and all the flora. I think in cognitive form under the stars and the moon, and I exist with all human beings in my domain, but 'tis thee that conveys the ultimate ontology in my cognition.

GOD: Remember thy place on Earth with thy kind and all that exists under the heavens, remember well and take heed, let thy judgement determine life on Earth.

MAN: I am a human being, living on Earth as thy guest, living on Earth for such an infinitesimal span of time, living on Earth and struggling with morality, living on Earth with the knowledge of mortality, living on Earth without tangible proof of thine existence.

GOD: Thou question my creation of thee and seek answers to my existence?

MAN: Nay, I fear for my existence and all of my kind. We use the finite Earth to survive and multiply. But I question the meaning of life and the mystery after death.

GOD: 'Tis true, by all the light in the heavens and on Earth, and by all the creation from the beginning to the end, thou shall never know.

MAN: 'Tis my existence, under the dust and the breath, and by all the universe from matter unto void, 'tis my fate.

THE REASON

I

Everyone stepped forward behind the light,
Expecting a conclusion from the sun,
Expecting too much from every human being on Earth,
Relying on everyone for the answers,
Waiting behind flesh and blood or the gray horizon.

II

Someone stepped forward behind the light,
Expecting a conclusion from everyone,
Expecting too much from a human being,
Relying on someone for the answers,
Waiting behind every human on Earth or the dense horizon.

III

No one stepped forward behind the light,
No conclusion was ever made,
No human being expected the answers,
No one relied on every human being,
No one waited for the ultimate question
Or the absent light from the transparent sun.

IV

I stepped forward behind the intense yellow light,
Expecting a conclusion from the new moon,
Expecting too much from every human being on Earth,
Relying on my heartbeat,
Waiting impatiently below the horizon
For the answer and for my tranquil heart.

THE APPLE IN MIDAIR

The question of infinity or the finite answer,
And the tree was isolated from all humans and all fauna,
And I empathized with the roots and the leaves,
Standing behind the bark and the skin,
Observing the gravity between the limb and the dirt,
Or ascertaining the difference between humans and flora,
But the computation was false,
The descent was between the limb and the dirt or the sky and the seed,
And the question of measurement became an estimation
As the leaves settled temporarily on the dirt
And the air filled with matter and void,
A constant absence of balance between humans and reality,
But the computation was an opinion,
A question of finite proportions or human limitations,
And I empathized with the mathematical length,
Standing behind the roots and the leaves,
Observing the loneliness between the limb and the dirt,
Or ascertaining the difference between loneliness and isolation,
Or the boundary of the fruitful tree.

THE SIVATHERIUM ON THE LIQUID PLAINS

They accused me of living on Earth,
Inhaling the air,
And looking up at the stars,
They accused the insects of being superabundant,
But the heavy rain continued and society complained about the desert
climate,
Or they accused civilization of not recognizing the obviousness in society,
But I recognized the foothills and the humid air,
A great distance in time from conjecture to conclusion,
Or an instant in time between supposition and speculation,
And I accused myself in the reflection,
A puddle on the geographical space,
A period of time not in human memory,
But they recognized the states of matter,
The wet plateau and the arid ground,
Or they argued over the formula between society and civilization,
A disagreement on the same level,
But I remembered the hillock and the primitive atmosphere,
Watching the selected few search for ossicones and seashells,
Watching the wind disintegrate the sand impressions
Of promegantereon and megantereon.

A PHILOSOPHICAL POEM FOR A UNIVERSAL MIND

And the heartbeat ceased below the sunlight,
A stillness below the glare,
And I thought I was in the proximity of space and time,
To be near or close to the farthest point,
Or to think and understand about the upturned earth
Between fertilization and ash,
Or to think and understand about the light-year and the molecular clock
With the exact proximity
Between conception and dust,
So I thought about my consciousness and the question of my objective
existence.

2014 – 2017